My family celebrates
Id-ul-Fitr

Cath Senker

Photography by Chris Fairclough

W

FRANKLIN WATTS
LONDON • SYDNEY

First published in 2009 by
Franklin Watts
338 Euston Road
London NW1 3BH

Franklin Watts Australia
Level 17/207 Kent Street
Sydney NSW 2000

ISBN: 978 0 7496 9059 5

Dewey classification number: 297.3'6

A CIP catalogue record for this book is available
from the British Library.

Planning and production by Discovery Books Limited
Editor: Laura Durman
Designer: Ian Winton
Photography by Chris Fairclough

The author and photographer would like to thank the following for their help in preparing this book:
Altaf, Shahla, Hajra, Iman and Malaika Razak; Ameera, Abdullah and Ahmed Razak; Amna and
Aisha Shabbir; Imam Muhammad Al-Shibli and the worshippers of Al-Quds mosque, Brighton.

Please note, the way that people celebrate festivals varies and this book represents the experience of
one family. It should not be assumed that everyone celebrates in the same way.

Printed in China

Franklin Watts is a division of Hachette Children's Books, an Hachette UK company.
www.hachette.co.uk

Words that appear in **bold** in the text are explained in the glossary.

Contents

Globe panels

People celebrate Id-ul-Fitr in lots of different ways around the world. Look out for the globe panels for some examples.

About my family and me

I'm called Iman and I am 7 years old. My older sister Hajra is 11, and my younger sister Malaika is 6. Malaika and I enjoy drawing and painting. Hajra loves reading.

Here is my family outside our house. I'm dressed in pink.

74

We're a close family. My grandma lives with us. I have aunts, uncles and cousins living nearby, too. I often play with my cousins.

Mum and Dad's families come from Pakistan and we're Muslims. We pray at home and learn about **Islam**. This book will show you how my family celebrates **Id-ul-Fitr**.

This is me with my sisters. Hajra is in the middle and Malaika is on the right.

The end of Ramadan

Id-ul-Fitr is a festival at the end of **Ramadan**, the month of **fasting**. In Ramadan, older children and adults do not eat or drink during the daytime. They eat a small meal early in the morning before it is light.

When it is dark again, they break their fast with a light snack. Later, they eat an evening meal.

Mum and Hajra break the fast in the evening with some dates and milk.

Morocco

In Morocco, people usually break the fast with a filling, spicy soup called harira. Then they enjoy sweet mint tea, dates and cakes made with honey or almonds.

During Ramadan, Muslims spend time reading the **Qur'an**. Dad is reading a **surah** with my cousins Ahmed (left) and Abdullah.

Id-ul-Fitr begins

Near the end of Ramadan, we prepare for Id. We clean and decorate the house and make Id cards.

I make Id cards with Malaika and our cousins, Amna, Aisha and Ahmed.

When people see the **new moon**, the month of Ramadan is over. The day after is called Id. We ring the **mosque** to check when Id will be.

Pakistan

People do not know exactly which day will be Id. In Pakistan, some people stand on the flat roof of their houses and gaze at the sky, hoping to spot the new moon.

On the morning of Id, we all wake up very early.

I put up pretty Id decorations with Hajra.

Going to the mosque

Hajra, Malaika and I have the day off school for Id. We say our prayers. Then we put on beautiful, new clothes.

National holiday

The day of Id is a holiday in many Muslim countries, including Indonesia, Saudi Arabia and Pakistan. Muslims gather in mosques and large outdoor spaces. There are prayers from early morning until night-time.

I pray at home with Mum.

It is important for Muslims to pray together at Id. In our family, only my dad goes to the mosque to pray. I say prayers at home with my sisters and my mum.

Some women and girls go to the mosque, though. They pray separately from the men and boys.

Dad greets the **imam** at the mosque. He says 'As-Salamu-Alaykum', which means 'Peace be upon you.'

In the mosque

Lots of people go to the mosque at Id. They perform special Id prayers together and give thanks to **Allah**.

My cousins, Ahmed and Abdullah (front right), worship at the mosque with other men and boys.

The imam gives a **khutbah** (sermon). He talks about how people can become better Muslims.

The imam gives his khutbah.

Xingjiang, China

Xingjiang is the region of China with the largest number of Muslims. About 10 million people celebrate Id! Hundreds of people go to a mosque in Urumqi, the capital of Xingjiang. After the prayers, the party begins. The men perform a festive folk dance, to the beat of drums.

Happy Id!

After the prayers, people greet each other with hugs. They say 'Id Mubarak', which means 'Happy Id'. Id is a time to be kind to others. People forgive each other for things they have done wrong.

Dad greets friends coming out of the mosque. They say 'Id Mubarak' to each other.

Before the festival, we give some money to the mosque. It is called **Zakat-ul-Fitr**. The mosque shares the money out among poor people. This means that everyone can celebrate Id.

We have a charity box at home. Before Id, my sisters and I save up to give Zakat-ul-Fitr.

Special food

In the days before Id, Mum and Grandma were busy cooking special food.

After prayers at the mosque, my aunts, uncles and cousins come to our house.

We welcome our cousins Ameera and Abdullah.

Malaysia

In Ipoh in Malaysia, people gather with friends and family to eat a special meal of sticky rice cooked in **bamboo** stems.

We eat a tasty lunch of Pakistani dishes. The adults and older children have been fasting. For the first time in a month, they can eat a meal during the day.

Yogurt salad

Sweet rice

Seviyan

Pilau rice with meat

Chicken tikka

For Id lunch, we have meat, rice and salad. After, we eat **seviyan**, a sweet pudding. It's my favourite dish.

Gifts

Children are lucky at Id. Our parents give us new clothes and presents. This year, Mum and Dad give me a lovely sleepover kit and Malaika has one, too.

My grandma gives us each some Id money.

Bangladesh

In the countryside in Bangladesh, there are Id fairs. People can buy pottery, musical instruments and sweets. At some fairs, there are merry-go-rounds and puppet shows for children.

Hajra fasted for all of Ramadan. She's helpful and works hard at school, so Dad gives her a special present. It's a new laptop computer!

After we open our presents, we visit other people to wish them a happy Id. Id is a fantastic day!

Hajra is really pleased with her new laptop.

An Id-ul-Fitr recipe: seviyan

Here's how we make seviyan for Id-ul-Fitr. Why don't you ask an adult to help you to make it?

1. Heat the butter in a pan and fry the **vermicelli** noodles until they are light brown.

You will need

- 1 tablespoon butter
- 50g vermicelli noodles
- $\frac{1}{2}$ litre full-cream milk
- 200g condensed milk
- 2 cardamom pods, powdered
- 2 tablespoons almonds and pistachio nuts (if you want)

2. Boil the full-cream milk in a different pan.

3. Add the condensed milk, vermicelli noodles, cardamom powder and nuts to the milk.

4. Cook for 2 to 3 minutes, until the noodles are soft.

5. Carefully spoon the seviyan into bowls and serve hot.

Serviyan - the finished dish.

Glossary

Allah The Muslim name for God.

bamboo A tall plant often used to make furniture. The young plants can be eaten.

chicken tikka An Indian and Pakistani chicken dish. The chicken is baked in the oven with yoghurt and spices.

fasting Going without food or drink for religious reasons.

Id-ul-Fitr A Muslim festival. It can also be spelled Id ul-Fitr or Eid ul-Fitr.

imam The person who leads the prayers in the mosque.

Islam The religion of Muslims.

khutbah A speech made by the imam at special times, such as at Friday prayers and Id.

mosque The Muslim place of worship.

new moon When the moon appears in the sky as a very thin crescent shape.

pilau rice Rice cooked with onions and spices.

Qur'an The Muslims' holy book.

Ramadan The Muslim month of fasting. Muslims go without food and drink during the daytime, for religious reasons.

seviyan A sweet, milky pudding eaten at Id-ul-Fitr.

surah A chapter of the Qur'an.

vermicelli Very thin strands of pasta, used to make seviyan.

Zakat-ul-Fitr Money that Muslims give before Id to help poor people.

Finding out more

Books
Ramadan and Id-ul-Fitr by Rosalind Kerven (Evans Brothers, 2004)
We Love Id-ul-Fitr by Saviour Pirotta (Wayland, 2006)
Why Is This Festival Special? Id-ul-Fitr by Jillian Powell (Franklin Watts, 2005)

DVD/CD-Rom
A child's eye view of festivals, produced by Child's Eye Media.
   This DVD introduces children to different festivals, including Id-ul-Fitr.
Our Places of Worship, produced by Wayland.
   This CD-Rom explores six major religions found in Britain. Each religion is
   introduced by a child who follows the faith.

Websites
http://www.britishcouncil.org/kids-stories-favourite-day-eid.htm
   On the British Council website, you can listen to a child talking about Id-ul-Fitr.
http://www.woodlands-junior.kent.sch.uk/Homework/religion/muslimfestivals.htm
   This website contains information about different Muslim festivals.

For teachers
http://www.reonline.org.uk/allre/tt_nframe.php?http://www.teachers.tv/video/1449
   Teacher's Guide to Islam – video of a family at Id-ul-Fitr, which also explains the
   basic ideas of Islam.

Note to parents and teachers: Every effort has been made by the Publishers to ensure that these websites are suitable for children, that they are of the highest educational value, and that they contain no inappropriate or offensive material. However, because of the nature of the Internet, it is impossible to guarantee that the contents of these sites will not be altered. We strongly advise that Internet access is supervised by a responsible adult.

Index